contents

To parents and teachers

This thesaurus is a collection of word lists relating to topics which children are likely to need in their written work.

Within their sections, the words are arranged by association of ideas rather than alphabetically. This is intended to give children additional help and to stimulate their thoughts on the topics about which they are writing.

The general vocabulary includes words which would not normally be found in children's vocabulary lists but which children easily recognise, often use in conversation, and sometimes include in their writing. Examples are *aqualung, cassette, roustabout, prescription, scampi, turbulence, tachograph* and *wetsuit*.

Included also are words that children recognise and use mainly in their shortened form. Examples of such words are *hi-fi, soccer, vet, fridge* and *artic*.

The vocabulary of this book also includes about seven per cent of words which are on the periphery of many children's vocabularies. They hear their parents or other adults use these words in association with particular circumstances. Though the children may not understand these words fully, they know of their association. Words of this kind have been deliberately included. Examples are *consultant, flexible, fluorescent, sympathetic* and *emergency*.

Many of the sections in the thesaurus have simple cross-references to other sections, so that a child is always given the opportunity of finding the maximum number of words associated with the topic on which he or she is writing. For example, the word *doctor* (in the section on 'Work') is given a direct and simple cross-reference to the section on **health**, where words associated with a doctor's duties are given. Similarly, the section on **indoor games** is cross-referenced with **toyshop**, and so on. There are approximately three hundred of these cross-references.

Important

When using this thesaurus a child will sometimes find a group of helpful words among which there is one word about whose meaning he or she is not sure. He or she should be encouraged to look up this word in a dictionary.

How to use this book

This book can be used in two ways to find the word you want.

The first way

To find a word that you have forgotten (it may be on the tip of your tongue!), look at the Contents pages. Look through the headings and find the most suitable one. Under that heading, find the section which seems likely to contain words on the subject you are writing about. Note its section number. Find that section in the main part of the book. In that section you will find the word you want, or a word like it.

For example, suppose you have forgotten the name given to your big, back teeth. Look at the Contents pages under the word **health**. There you will find that the section on **dentist** has the number 36. Find section 36 in the main part of the book and there you will find the word you want, which is **molars**.

The second way

Sometimes when you are writing, you need to use a word very similar to one you have already used. You do not want to repeat the word you have used, but you cannot think of another one like it.

This time look in the index at the end of the book. Find the word you have already used. It will have a section number after it. Find that section in the main part of the book and it will contain other words which have similar meanings.

For example, suppose that you have already used the word **annoyed** but you now want another word which means almost the same. Find **annoyed** in the index. You will see that the word **annoyed** has the section number 52 after it.

Find section 52 in the main part of the book. There you will find other words which have meanings similar to the word **annoyed**, such as **displeased**.

Important

If you see a word that you would like to use, but you are not quite sure of its real meaning, *look it up in your dictionary*.

Contents of the thesaurus with section numbers

Contents of the thesaurus with section numbers

Contents of the thesaurus with section numbers

Contents of the thesaurus with section numbers

THESAURUS

personal

1

family
mother
father
parents
single parent
husband
wife
brother
half-brother
sister
half-sister
twins
son
step-son
daughter
step-daughter
grandparents
grandmother
grandfather
grandchild
granddaughter
grandson
ancestor
descendant

relation
brother-in-law
sister-in-law
mother-in-law
father-in-law

3

birth
baby
born
birthday

4

marriage
bachelor
spinster
engaged
ring
married
wedding
bride

bridegroom
bridesmaid
best man
church —
service
registry office
reception
party
invitation
guests
honeymoon
separated
divorced

5

death
died
funeral
buried
cemetery
cremated
crematorium

2

relatives
uncle
aunt
nephew
niece
cousin

6

friends
friendship
best friend
playmate
partner
companion
mate
comrade
team-mate
helper
supporter
neighbour

home

7

house (outside)

detached
semi-detached
terrace
bungalow
flat
apartment
cottage
caravan
mobile home
veranda
conservatory
porch
garage
coalplace
path
pavement
wall
fence
hedge
gate
roof
slates
tiles
thatch
chimney
TV aerial
gutter
fall-pipe

downspout
drain
yard
patio
stone
brick
window
double-glazed
french window
patio door
entrance
door
doorstep
knocker
knob
ring
letter box

8

house (inside)

carpet
rug
mat
lino
tiles
skirting board
light
lamp
switch
curtains
net
blind
decoration
wallpaper
radiator

9

downstairs
hall
cloakroom
utility room
lobby
passage
coat-hook
mirror
stairs
banisters
handrail
dining-room
table
chairs
tablecloth
place-mats
sideboard
trolley
sitting-room
lounge
armchair
easy-chair
settee
couch
sofa
divan
three-piece suite
cushion
bookcase
cabinet
china
glass
shelf
shelves
ornament

vase
clock
hearth
fireplace
grate
mantlepiece
fender
poker
tongs
coal scuttle
gas fire
electric fire
picture
photograph
piano
television
radio
video
stereo
music centre
home computer
telephone
[see 164, 168, 290, 291]

10

kitchen
fitted kitchen
cooker
hob
electric
gas
stove
oven
microwave
grill

hotplate
burner
refrigerator
fridge
freezer
dishwasher
washing-machine
tumble-drier
sink
unit
waste-disposal unit
tap
mixer tap
drainer
cupboard
stool
worktop
work surface
scullery
pantry
larder
boiler
oil
solid fuel
central heating
thermostat
radiators

11

utensils
pans
pots
kettle
cutlery
crockery
dishes

contd.

tray
toaster
blender
food processor
grinder
bread
cutting board

12

bedroom
single bed
double bed
mattress
blanket
sheet
duvet
continental quilt
eiderdown
bedspread
pillow
bolster
cot
bunks
dressing-table
mirror
wardrobe
chest of drawers
tallboy
[see 164]

13

bathroom
bath
bathmat

shower
washbasin
toilet
bidet
mirror
nailbrush
facecloth
soap
toothbrush
toothpaste
glass
shampoo
bubble bath
towels
airing cupboard
loofah
sponge
brush
seat
flush
paper

14

loft
attic
storage
water tank
cistern
immersion heater
pipes
lagging
fibreglass
insulation

15

garden
soil
earth
plant
flower
shrub
vegetable
grass
lawn
sandpit
swing
paddling pool
washing-line
weeds
manure
peat
compost heap
fertiliser
toolshed
lean-to
lawnmower
hovermower
spade
fork
rake
hoe
cold frame
greenhouse
watering-can
hosepipe
spray
wheelbarrow
[see 138, 271]

school

16
building
entrance
steps
playground
hall
classroom
staffroom
school office
head's room
corridor
stairs
library
music room
kitchen
dining-room
boiler-house
swimming pool
playing field
garden
hut
[see 100-104]

17
adults
head teacher
headmistress
headmaster
deputy head
teacher
secretary
caretaker
cleaner

dinner lady
supervisor
cook
gardener
parents
[see 100-104]

18
classroom
blackboard
chalk
duster
desk
lid
seat
chair
table
cupboard
shelf
rack
clock

bookcase
sink
tap
cloth
books
pen
ink
pencil
biro
crayon
rubber
ruler

19
class
form
group
team
register
reading

contd.

composition
essay
exercise
question
answer
spelling
dictation
grammar
punctuation
sentence
phrase
clause
word
comma
full stop
capital letter
paragraph
work
mark
test
examination
report

writing
copy
lesson
period
break
timetable
bell
term
holiday
children
pupils
older
younger

cassette recorder
record-player
wall map
wall chart
globe
picture
illustration
textbook
exercise book
[see 100]

school subjects

20

educational aids
television
video recorder
radio
tape recorder

21

English
story
play
poem

22

mathematics
arithmetic
sums
add
subtract
multiply
divide
numbers
figures
fractions
decimals

23 science

calculate
calculator
computer
tables
ruler
shape
square
circle
rectangle
triangle
measurement
estimate
graph
metre
centimetre
litre
gram
kilogram
kilometre
tonne

23

science
experiment
test
apparatus
observe
measure
result
magnet
lens
magnifier
thermometer
burner
battery
scientist

24

history
time
past
old
ancient
prehistoric
date
event
battle
king
queen
prince
crusade
coat-of-arms
armour
chain-mail
helmet
horse
castle
defend
siege
dungeon
serf
conquer
civil war
parliament
republic

25

historical periods
prehistoric
Roman
Saxon

Dark Ages
Norman
Plantagenet
Tudor
Stuart
Hanoverian
Victorian
Edwardian
modern

26

geography
atlas
map
scale
chart
globe
country
capital
island
sea
ocean
coast
north
south
east
west
pole
equator
hill
mountain
river
lake
channel
canal
seaport

contd.

products
raw materials
industries
transport
[see 215]

27

art
brush
paint
paper
water
colour
pencil
draw
sketch
scene
sculpture
pattern
collage
mobile
crayon
pastel
shadow

28

craft
clay
Plasticine
paper
cardboard
balsa wood
string

scissors
knife
fold
crease
bend
score
cut
stick
paste
glue
model
design

29

needlework
knitting
needles
pins
wool
woollen
cast on
cast off
purl
plain
rib
material
thread
sew
sewing-machine
stitch
tack
hem
seam
embroider

30

physical education
P.E.
dance
run
chase
hop
jump
vault
handstand
cartwheel
somersault
astride
climb
wall bars
vest
shorts
pumps
plimsolls
rope
ball
catch
game
playing field
pitch
court
team

31

music
singing
piano
pianist
voice
solo

choir
recorder
play
violin
guitar
amplifier
notes
concert
instrument
sheet music
band
orchestra

health

32

general
healthy
fit
well
vigorous
robust
strong
unhealthy
ill
sick
unwell
feverish
ailing
feeble
frail
delicate
check-up
diet
[see 67]

33

disease
illness
germ
virus
epidemic
antibiotics
disinfectant
septic
antiseptic
temperature
thermometer
injection
immunise
vaccination
needle
stomach-ache
cough
cold
flu
influenza
tonsilitis
mumps

measles
chicken pox
bronchitis
whooping cough
asthma
hay fever

34

accident
ambulance
stretcher
police
oxygen
kiss of life
broken
fracture
X-ray
operation
theatre
surgeon
anaesthetic
unconscious
contd.

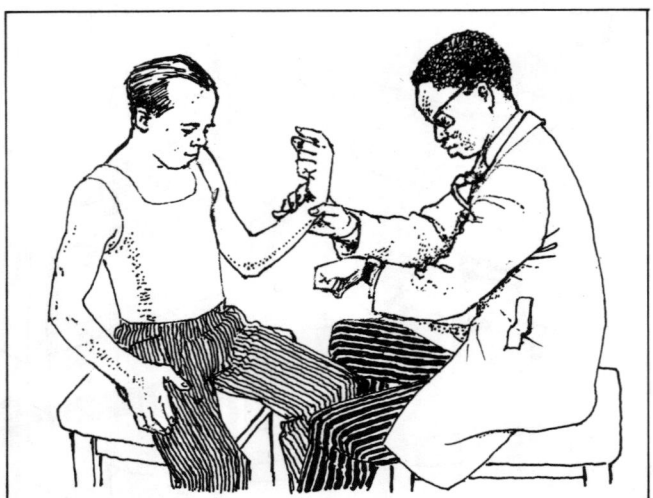

hospital
ward
nurse
patient
bandage
plaster cast
visitor
convalescent
[see 81]

35

doctor
surgery
waiting-room
stethoscope
specialist
consultant
clinic
blood-test
treatment
injection
prescription
chemist

medicine
ointment
pills
tablets
lotion
[see 78-82]

36

dentist
dental surgeon
surgery
chair
couch
teeth
gums
molars
examine
injection
numb
filling
drill
extraction
[see 80]

37

body
head
scalp
hair
forehead
temple
face
ear
eye
eyelid
eyelash
pupil
iris
lens
retina
nose
nostril
cheek
mouth
lip
tongue
teeth
neck
trunk
shoulder
chest
arm
leg
joint
elbow
knee
wrist
ankle
hand
thumb

finger
nail
knuckle
palm
foot
instep
toe
muscle

38

organs
lung
heart
beat
blood
artery
vein
stomach
liver
kidney
intestine
digestion

39

bones
skeleton
skull
jaw
collar-bone
shoulder-blade
rib
breast-bone
ribcage
backbone

spine
vertebrae
disc
hip
pelvis
thigh-bone
shin-bone
kneecap

40

positions
stand
sit
lie
lean
sprawl
recline
squat
lounge

41

movements (slow)
linger
loiter
dawdle
crawl
creep
toddle
waddle
amble
hobble
hop
limp

saunter
plod
shuffle
shamble
slither
stagger
lurch
stumble
totter
topple
trudge
stroll

42

movements (fast)
stride
march
trot
run
hurry
scurry
scamper
charge
rush
hurtle
sprint
chase
skip
dance
romp
dart
caper
jump
leap
spring
fall

senses

43
sight (bright)
blinding
brilliant
shiny
clear
visible
readable
transparent
glossy
gleaming
reflection
alight
ablaze
luminous
radiant
glowing
fluorescent
glaring
sparkling
glittering
dazzling
flashing
twinkling

44
sight (dull)
faint
opaque
dim
misty
cloudy
foggy
blurred
shady
unlit
dark
indistinct
unreadable
invisible

45
hearing (loud)
ear-splitting
deafening
noise
roar
bang
crash
explosion
thunder
boom
echo
din
rumble
clang
slam
clash
ring
clamour
clatter
resound
uproar
creak
crunch
splash

46
hearing (quiet)
peaceful
tranquil
lull
hushed
faint
dumb
mute
inaudible
soundless
soundproof
noiseless
silence

47
smell
odour
aroma
tang
smelly
foul
stuffy
stink
stench
reek
rank
musty
offensive
overpowering
suffocating
acrid
fetid
pungent
clean

fragrant
fragrance
fresh
perfume
sweet
scented

48

touch
soft
downy
velvety
smooth
polished
glossy
slippery
flexible
pliable
flabby
springy
hairy
clammy
greasy
oily
sticky
slimy
wet
hard
firm
solid
rough
coarse
uneven
jagged
wrinkled

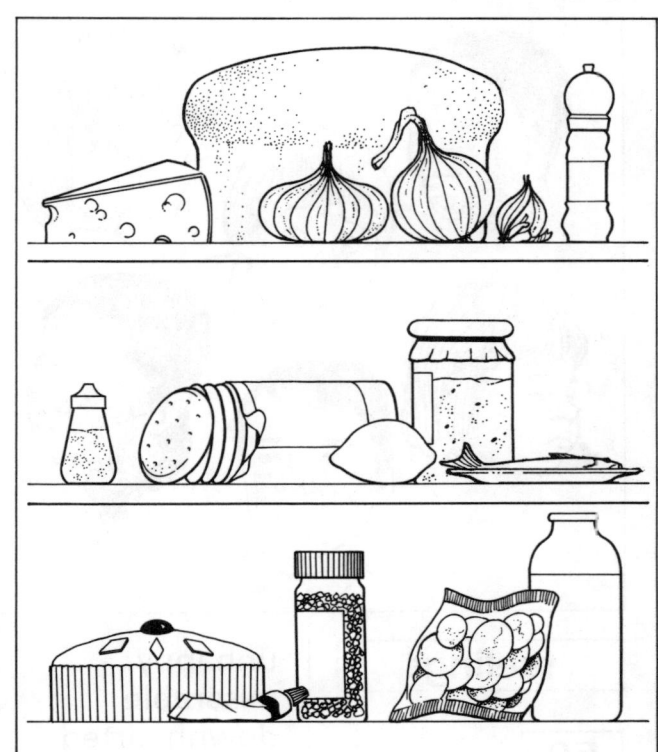

sharp
brittle
crumbling
prickly
lumpy
thick
thin

49

taste
tasty
sweet
rich
sickly
sour
acid

sharp
salty
savoury
hot
stale
tasteless
bland
insipid
luscious
spicy
tart
bitter
strong
mild
delicious
appetising
palatable

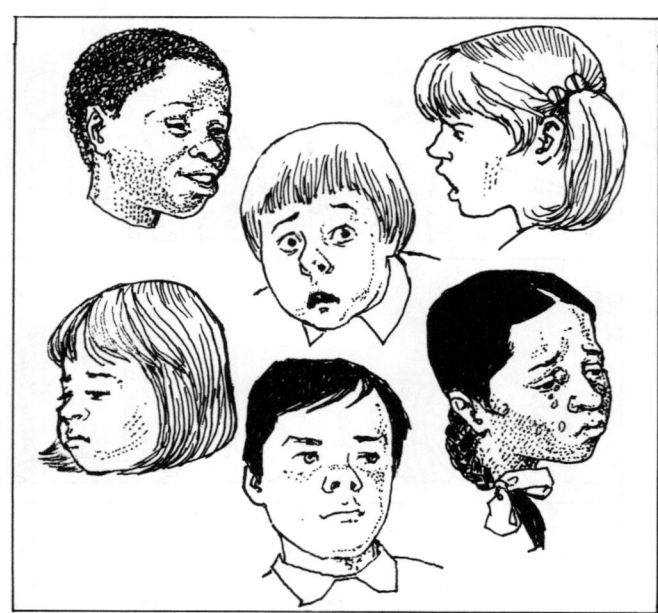

annoyed
furious
vexed
displeased
irritated
discontented

53

fear
afraid
frightened
scared
terrified
fearful
worried
horrified
anxious
uneasy
timid
cowardly

feelings

50

pleasure
pleased
happy
glad
excited
joyful
delighted
satisfied
contented
cheerful
gratified

unhappy
miserable
downhearted
heartbroken
dismal
downcast
discouraged
distressed
mournful
sorrowful
gloomy
dejected
depressed
grief-stricken

52

anger
cross
fed-up
angry

54

courage
brave
bold
daring
plucky
adventurous
fearless
valiant
courageous
heroic
cool

51

sadness
sad
sorry

55

excitement
excited
eager
thrilled
enthusiastic
elated
aroused
inspired
turned-on

56

interest
interested
curious
fascinated
attracted
attentive
gripped
captivated
sympathetic

57

boredom
bored
tired
weary
listless
uninterested
lackadaisical

clothing

58

outer
coat
overcoat
anorak
cagoule
duffel coat
wind-cheater
mackintosh
raincoat
gloves
mittens
legwarmers
suit
jacket
blazer
tunic
waistcoat
pocket
overalls

59

trunk and legs
shirt
sleeve
cuff
T-shirt
blouse
sweater
pullover
jumper

jersey
cardigan
dress
gown
skirt
kilt
smock
swimsuit
trunks
bikini
trousers
jeans
denims
dungarees
shorts
belt
buckle
braces
socks
stockings
tights

60

feet
pair
shoes
boots
wellingtons
pumps
plimsolls
sandals
trainers
slippers

61

underwear
vest
singlet
pants
knickers
briefs
bra
nightdress
pyjamas
dressing gown
housecoat

62

head
hat
cap
beret
hood
turban

63

neck
scarf
collar
shawl
muffler
tie
tie-pin
bow-tie
cravat

64

fasteners
button
buttonhole
zip fastener
Velcro
press-stud
hook and eye
laces
ribbon
brooch
clasp
clip
toggle

65

babywear
nappy
shawl
baby-gro
bonnet
bootees
mittens
matinee coat

66

materials
cotton
wool
tweed
velvet
cord
silk
nylon

Terylene
Crimplene
polyester

people

67

build
tall
lanky
short
small
fat
plump
lean
thin
slim
slender
sturdy
thickset
brawny
muscular
powerful
robust
strong
trim
dainty
tiny
puny
frail
delicate
gaunt
bent
disabled
deformed
[see 32]

68

complexion
pale
fair
freckles
dark
sallow
swarthy
bronzed
dusky
ruddy
tanned
sunburnt
wrinkled
weatherbeaten

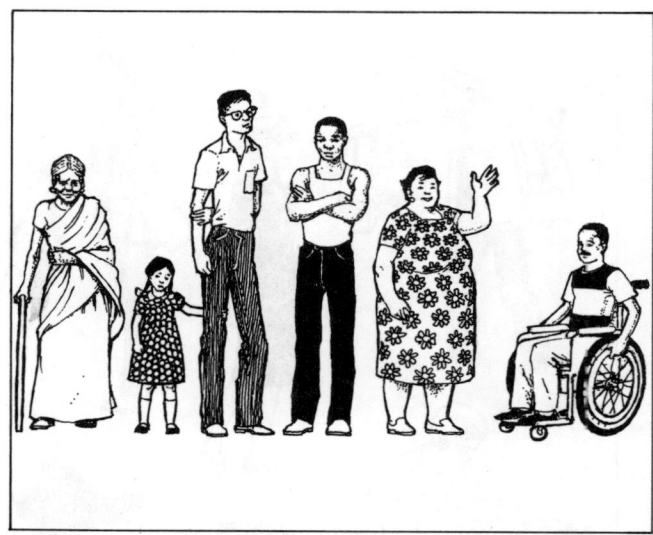

69

hair
blond(e)
golden
fair
black
brown
mousey
auburn
grey
white
wavy
straight
curly
plaited
tousled
tangled
bald
beard

moustache
sideboards
sideburns
[see 119]

70

character
pleasant
charming
courteous
friendly
sympathetic
affectionate
cheerful
humorous
reliable
dependable
sincere
kind
gentle
loving
truthful

honest
fair
unselfish
shy
reserved
unpleasant
wicked
cruel
selfish
unkind
mean
sly
cunning
jealous
quarrelsome
ungrateful
stern
boastful
arrogant
proud
stubborn
deceitful
conceited

73

post
post office
sorting office
letters
parcels
stamps
collection
delivery
postbox
pillar box
mail van
[see 161, 293]

74

coal
coalyard
coke
anthracite
smokeless fuel
sacks
scales
pit
colliery
winding gear
miner
[see 114, 133]

71

appearance
delightful
clean
fashionable
smart
neat
elegant
dull
drab
shabby
tattered
dirty
untidy
unkempt

work

72

milk
roundsman
delivery
dairy
cream
yogurt
bottle
carton
float
tanker
farm
[see 155]

75

refuse
refuse truck
refuse tip
rubbish

bin
waste bin
bin bag
litter
dustman

76

police
policewoman
police station
sergeant
constable
inspector
detective
superintendent
uniform
helmet
whistle
radio
truncheon
beat
[see 296]

77

fire
fireman
fire-station
fire-engine
appliance
siren
helmet
axe
hose

hydrant
water
ladder
turntable
fireguard
fire-extinguisher
fire-blanket
[see 279]

78

ambulance
depot
driver
stretcher
first-aid
emergency
oxygen
flashers
siren
hospital
[see 34]

79

doctor
health centre
surgery
waiting room
examination
stethoscope
treatment
prescription
[see 35]

80

dentist
surgery
chair
couch
teeth
examine
injection
numb
drill
filling
extraction
[see 36]

81

nurse
clinic
hospital
matron
sister
staff nurse
midwife
district nurse
[see 34]

82

chemist
dispense
medicine
bandage
pills
tablets
ointment
bottles
jars

contd.

prescription
[see 162]

83

vet
veterinary surgeon
surgery
animals
pets
examination
treatment
operation
[see 261, 262]

84

shop
assistant
counter
goods
stock
display
service
self-service
till
money
[see 177-182]

85

newsagent
newspapers
magazines
sweets
cigarettes
tobacco

86

buses
driver
conductor
one-man bus
pay-as-you-enter
exact fare
route
bell
stop
ticket
token
[see 227]

87

trucks
lorry
van
load
route
destination
delivery
transport café
meal
rest
radio
tachograph
[see 227, 235]

88

trains
locomotive
coach
guard
journey

ticket-collector
controls
signals
station
unmanned station
level-crossing
siding
[see 239, 242]

89

joiner
carpenter
wood
beams
boards
frames
joints
saw
hammer
nails
screwdriver
screws
drill
[see 136]

90

surveyor
poles
sighting
theodolite
levels
measuring
measurement
plan
map

91

architect
architecture
office
drawing-board
perspective
drawing
plans
model
style
[see 226]

92

building
building site
foundations
walls
floor
roof
windows
double glazing
doors
stairs
path
[see 226]

93

bricklayer
mortar
trowel
spirit-level
stringline
conveyor
hod
[see 7, 226]

94

plumber
pipes
blowlamp
boiler
water tank
cistern
toilet
taps
overflow
freeze
burst
leak
flood
[see 7]

95

painter
brushes
scraper

blowlamp
primer
undercoat
gloss paint
non-drip
emulsion
ladder
[see 7]

96

decorator
wallpaper
paste
scissors
table
hang
plumbline
pattern
match
drybrush
[see 7]

joint
leak
smell
repair
meter

100

teacher
class
children
blackboard
desk
books
marking
correction
help
homework
[see 16-32]

97

electrician
electricity
circuit
switch
wires
connect
current
socket
plug
fuse
meter
shock
spark
[see 7, 167]

98

mechanic
spanner
wrench
drill
bolt
gauge
weld
blowtorch
[see 232, 233]

99

gas fitter
pipes
join

101

head teacher
headmistress
headmaster
office
interview
assembly
[see 16-32]

102

cook
kitchen
stoves
ovens
prepare

meals
roast
boil
grill
fry
[see 16]

103

caretaker
boiler-room
heating
fuel
oil
coke
keys
doors
locks
gate
windows
ladder
repairs
[see 16, 137]

104

cleaner
vacuum cleaner
brush
duster
cloth
mop
sponge
soap
water
disinfectant
[see 16, 137]

105

editor
publisher
journalist
reporter
news
newspaper
articles
magazines
books
edit
deadline
[see 294]

106

printer
paper
ink
type
colour
setting
proofs
machines
folding
cutting
[see 194, 294]

107

lawyer
office
clerk
brief
solicitor
client
case

documents
[see 297]

108

judge
magistrate
barrister
court
oath
defence
defendant
prosecution
witness
accused
prisoner
jury
verdict
innocent
guilty
sentence
appeal
prison
[see 297, 298]

109

engineer
mechanic
fitter
workshop
machines
bench
lathe
drill
cutter
[see 136]

110

military
soldier
sailor
airman
marine
war
fight
attack
defend

111

docks
docker
ship
ferry
car ferry
roll-on
roll-off
load
unload
cargo
container
crane
fork-lift truck
warehouse
[see 243, 247]

112

shipbuilder
shipyard
crane
gantry
slipway

keel
hull
steel
plates
rivets
launch
[see 243, 247]

113

steelworker
ore
coke
blast furnace
molten
metal
ingots
power hammer
forging
casting

114

miner
colliery
mine
pit
shaft
hard hat
cage
seam
coalface
conveyor belt
pithead
baths
dirt

danger
[see 74, 133]

115

car worker
assembly-line
car-bodies
welding
electrics
assembling
bolts
nuts
spanners
screws
screwdriver
multiple
hinges
fitting
testing
spraying
polishing
[see 231, 232]

116

fisherman
boat
nets
trawl
seas
shoal
catch
storm
oilskins
radar

port
docks
[see 243-248]

117

seaman
ship
deck
ropes
hold
cargo
winch
derrick
storm
oilskins
radar
port
harbour
docks
[see 243-248]

118

oil-driller
roustabout
oil rig
hard hat
drills
pipes
platform
helipad
gusher
on-stream
[see 132]

119

hairdresser
scissors
comb
shampoo
set
style
permanent-wave
tint
dye
drier
blow-drier
[see 69, 173]

120

model
clothes
background

pose
camera
photograph
lighting
magazines

121

dressmaker
tailor
cloth
scissors
tape measure
pattern
sewing-machine
fitting
pressing
[see 174, 175]

125

computer programmer
computer operator
program
software
hardware
disc
screen
print-out

126

librarian
lending library
catalogue
author
fiction
non-fiction
reference
shelves
borrowing
[see 194]

122

secretary
typist
clerk
office
desk
typewriter
shorthand
notebook
file
ledger
photocopier

123

waitress
uniform
table
cutlery
crockery

glassware
tablecloth
tray
menu
order
courses
bill
[see 144, 154]

124

accountant
cashier
accounts
budget
income
expenditure
balance
calculator
computer
tax

127

farming
farmhouse
fields
arable
poultry
crops
machinery
ploughing
reaping
harvest
[see 142, 222]

128

shepherd
sheep
sheepdog
flock
ram
ewe
lamb
shearing
wool
[see 222]

129

labourer
spade
shovel
pick
dig
excavate
[see 230]

130

apprentice
apprenticeship
learning
training
practice
practising
study
examinations
qualify

power

131

electricity
power station
generator
turbine
dynamo
cables
pylons
distribution
[see 167]

132

oil
rig
drill
pipe
tanker
refinery
lubricating
paraffin
petrol
diesel
kerosene
[see 118]

133

coal
coalmine
pithead
screens
grades
hoppers

railways
wagons
coal trains
docks
power station
coalyard
[see 74, 114]

134

gas
North Sea
pipeline
gasholder
heating
cooking

135

nuclear power
atomic energy
reactor
water-cooled
gas-cooled
uranium
plutonium
radiation
danger

tools

136

bench
hammer
screwdriver

contd.

saw
chisel
spanner
mallet
plane
vice
brace and bit
pliers
pincers
drill
file
soldering iron
nail
screw
bolt
nut
washer
electric tools
[see 89, 98, 165]

137

domestic
broom
brush
dustpan
vacuum cleaner
mop
bucket
floorcloth
duster
feather duster
chamois leather
[see 103, 104]

138

garden
spade
fork
rake
hoe
trowel
shears
secateurs
lawnmower
rotavator
hedge clipper
hosepipe
broom
wheelbarrow
watering-can
water-butt
[see 15, 271]

139

electronics
calculator
computer
program
word processor
print-out
photocopier

140

computer
terminal
interface

floppy disc
cassette
byte
pixel
database
hardware
software
program
[see 125]

141

cooking
knife
fork
spoon
slice
can-opener
bottle-opener
mixer
blender
food processor
toaster
kettle
whisk
sieve
scales
rolling-pin
colander
scissors
basin
jug
pot
[see 10, 102, 152, 153]

142

farm
tractor
harrow
plough
roller
seeder
mower
hay-whisk
binder
combine harvester
stacker
potato-digger
silo
[see 127, 218, 222]

food

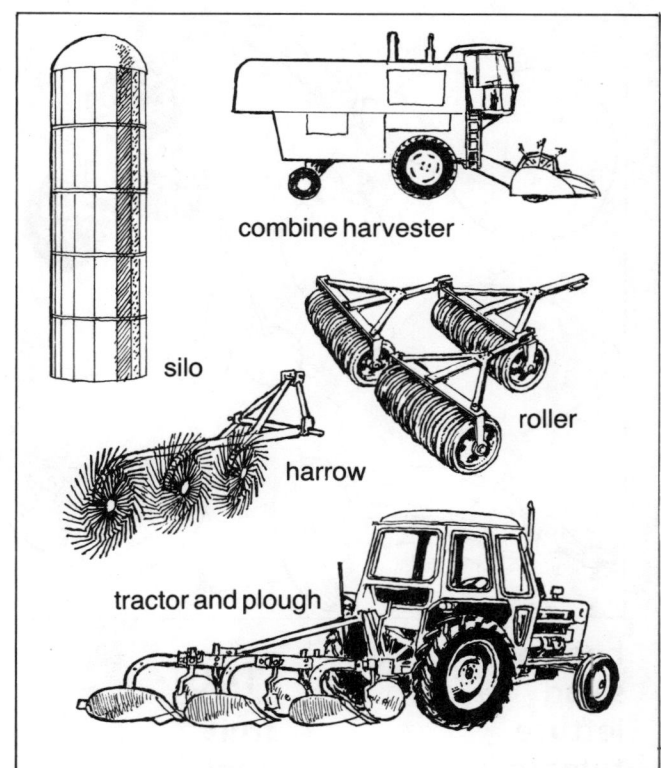

combine harvester

silo

roller

harrow

tractor and plough

143

nutrition
minerals
fats
carbohydrates
vitamins
calories
trace elements
protein

144

meals
eating
eat
ate

drink
drank
breakfast
lunch
tea
high tea
dinner
supper
dishes
main course
pudding
sweet
dessert
snack
take-away
[see 10, 49, 102, 123, 152, 153, 154]

145

vegetables
potatoes
crisps
chips
yam
peas
beans
cabbage
cauliflower
carrot
mango
turnip
swede
okra
parsnip

contd.

raisin
peach
apricot
plum
damson
prune
cherry
grape
melon
nectarine
tomato
avocado
kiwi fruit
peanut
hazel nut
walnut

beetroot
salad
lettuce
tomato
radish
cress
watercress
spinach
celery
cucumber
courgette
aubergine
sprouts
broccoli
leek
marrow
parsley
mint
garlic
sage
frozen vegetables

146

fruit
apple
pear
core
orange
satsuma
tangerine
peel
juicy
pips
banana
skin
lemon
pineapple
strawberry
raspberry
gooseberry
blackberry
currant

147

cereals
wheat
oats
barley
rye
corn
corn flakes
rice
rice crispies
bran
sago
tapioca
spaghetti
macaroni
mealie flour
[see 156, 157]

148

meat
bacon
lamb
mutton
beef
pork
ham
chicken
turkey
veal
rabbit
liver
kidney
tongue
sausage
salami
hamburger
beefburger
mince
minced beef
steak
chop
[see 158]

149

fish
fingers
paste
cod
haddock
hake
plaice
herring
kipper

sardine
salmon
tuna
whiting
sole
mackerel
crab
shrimp
prawn
scampi
lobster
oyster
[see 116, 267]

150

groceries
bread
loaf
loaves
butter
margarine
milk
cream
cheese
egg
yogurt
sugar
jam
syrup
honey
fat
lard
cooking-oil
salt
pepper
mustard

sauce
pickles
vinegar
[see 157]

151

beverages
tea
cocoa
milk shake
coffee
fruit juice
squash
minerals
pop
coke
[see 157]

152

cooking
cooked
boiled
fried
fry
roast
grilled
baked
stewed
poached
scrambled
mashed
minced
toasted
sandwich
omelette

contd.

pastry
gravy
[see 10, 102, 123, 153, 154]

153

confectionery
pie
tart
flan
cake
bun
muffin
scone
crumpet
biscuit
sponge
custard
jelly
ice cream
[see 156]

154

café
tables
cutlery
crockery
menu
condiments
sauces
waitress
order
service
bill

tip
tray
cafeteria
self-service
[see 123]

shops

155

dairy
milk
cream
butter
cheese
yogurt
eggs
bottles
cartons
packs
[see 72]

156

baker
flour
yeast
bread
loaf
loaves
buns
pies
cakes
tarts
[see 147, 153]

157

grocery
dry goods
beverages
cereals
preserves
tins
jars
packets
bottles
[see 147, 151]

158

butcher
meat
beef
lamb
pork
bacon
ham
veal
chicken
turkey
liver
kidney
sausage
minced beef
meat pie
[see 148]

159

sweetshop
sweets
chocolates

bars
blocks
toffee
pastilles
chewing gum
packets
bags
tubes
boxes

160
toyshop
doll
soldier
model
car
painting set
train set
doll's house
easel
game
scrap book
puzzle
skipping rope
bricks
[see 185, 186]

161
post office
stamps
letters
parcels
air mail
weight
scales
pension
licence
savings bank
[see 73, 293]

162
chemist
prescription
medicine
pills
tablets
ointment
bandage
cosmetics
powder
perfume
baby food
toilet articles
films
[see 82]

163
supermarket
wire basket
trolley
shelves
frozen food
checkout
till

164
furniture
table
chair
stool
easy-chair
rocking-chair
cupboard
bed
bunk
wardrobe

contd.

chest of drawers
dressing-table
tallboy
suite
settee
sofa-bed
carpet
rug
mat
[see 9, 12]

165

ironmonger
tools
utensils
pots
pans
bins
nails
screws
[see 136, 137]

166

florist
flowers
bunches
sprays
bouquets
wreaths
plants
pots
vases

167

electrics
bulbs
batteries
wire
cable
plugs
fuses
switches

connectors
[see 97, 131]

168

hi-fi
high-fidelity
radio tuner
amplifier
record-player
disc
L.P.
album
single
sleeve
tape recorder
cassette deck
mono
stereo
compact disc
programmer
digital recording
[see 290, 291]

169

television
TV set
screen size
remote control
teletext
rental
cable
video recorder
video cassette
[see 290, 291]

170

tobacconist
tobacco
pouch
packet
pipes
cigarettes
cigars
matches
lighters
fuel
flints
pipe-cleaners

171

department store
floors
basement
lift
escalator
assistant
cash-point
receipt
paper bag
carrier

172

card shop
greeting
birthday
engagement
anniversary
wedding
new baby

congratulations
Christmas
get well
retirement
condolence

173

hairdresser
ladies
gentlemen
hairstyle
shampoo
haircream
waves
perm
drier
curls
trim
haircut
[see 69, 119]

174

clothing (men's)
tailor
suits
trousers
jackets
overcoats
jumpers
socks
vest
pants
ties
hats

gloves
[see 58-66, 121]

175

clothing (women's)
dress
blouse
skirt
trousers
jumper
sweater
lingerie
underwear
tights
stockings
[see 58-66, 121]

176

wine store
off-licence
red wine
white wine
sparkling
champagne
rosé
sherry
port
whisky
gin
brandy
beer
lager
bottle
can
case

shopping

177
shops
manager
supervisor
assistant
cashier
buyer
helpful
polite
obliging
serve
queue
entrance
exit
opening hours
window display
counter
shelves
scales
weigh
[see 84]

178
market
open
stalls
covered
shops
pedestrian precinct
arcade
galleria
[see 84]

179
delivery
order
deposit
deliver
supply
stock
carton
crate
parcel
van
[see 84]

180
purchasing
purchase
shopping list
purse
wallet
pocket
money
bank notes
silver
copper
coins
pound
pence
cash
hire-purchase
H.P.
cheque
banker's card
credit card
till

pay
paid
V.A.T.
change
receipt
[see 84]

181
price
dear
expensive
cheap
inexpensive
bargain
offer
sale
reduced
discount
bill
buy
bought
purchase
coupon
stamps
receipt
credit note
refund
[see 84]

182
carrying
carry
carrier

carried
bag
basket
trolley
case
parcel
packet
package
paper
gift wrap
stick
tape
[see 84]

recreation

183

play
game
chase
dodge
catch
caught
race
run
running
follow-my-leader
hide and seek
dance
skip
rope
swing
jump
leapfrog

184

park
swings
roundabouts
slides
climbing frame
boating lake
ball
bat
field
pitch
net
court
racket
team
side
innings
turn
[see 225]

185

indoors
bricks
blocks
jigsaw
cards
dominoes
chess
draughts
ludo
Monopoly
puzzles
snap
soldiers
doll's house
marbles
darts
dartboard
skittles

contd.

conjurer
pop group
science fiction
[see 169, 290]

188

hi-fi
video recorder
videotape
record-player
tape recorder
compact disc player
C.D.
L.P.
single
cassette
tuner
speaker
[see 168, 291]

table-tennis
quoits
[see 160]

186

outdoors
bicycle
tricycle
scooter
pram
roller skates
ice-skates
skateboard
kite
fly
tent
climbing frame
paddling pool
[see 160, 184]

187

television
set
switch
remote control
picture
programme
Radio Times
TV Times
channel
cartoon
puppets
quizzes
western
detective
mystery
serial
musical
variety show
magician

189

theatre
stage
backstage
wings
curtain
lights
scenery
actors
play
comedy
tragedy
audience

clap
applause
programme
interval
pantomime
fairy godmother
principal boy
dame
villain
happy ending
exit

190

concert
hall
orchestra
band
choir
soloist
pianist
players
instruments
conductor
baton
symphony
concerto
chorus
organ
opera
ballet
mime
encore
ovation

191

cinema
box office
big screen
usherette
film
movie
stars
exciting
cartoon
special effects
soundtrack

192

circus
caravan
parade
big top
ring-master
acts
clowns
acrobats
horses
bareback riders
jugglers
trapeze artists
somersault
twist
catch
safety-net
tightrope
balance
animals
perform
hoops

cages
menagerie

193

fair
carnival
tents
roundabouts
rides
rifle shoot
prize
coconut-shies
helter-skelter
dodgems
stall
fortune-teller
bingo

194

books
picture
story
poetry
fairy tale
adventure
mystery
detective
animal
western
sport
science fiction
novel
play
paperback

contd.

fiction
non-fiction
information
school book
textbook
dictionary
encyclopaedia
volume
reference
historical
biography
autobiography
anthology
title
jacket
cover
page
chapter
contents
illustrations
notes
index
library
[see 105, 106]

sport

195

general
amateur
professional
league
city

county
national
international
championship
Olympics
record
winner
medal
match
team
players
opponents
referee
umpire
whistle
pitch
goal
crowd
spectators
supporters
score

196

football
soccer
association
strip
shirt
number
shorts
goalkeeper
defend
forward
striker
captain

linesman
flag
centre
corner
penalty
goal post
header
dribble
tackle
foul
free kick
nil
half-time
full-time
trainer
manager
substitute
home
away

197

rugby football
union
league
fifteen
thirteen
scrum
line-out
touch
try
dummy
tackle
penalty
points

198

cricket
ground
pitch
wicket
stumps
bails
new ball
bowler
over
run-up
spin
batsman
crease
runs
boundary
bye
fielder
wicket-keeper
gloves
pads
out
not out
catch
caught
stumped
run out
century
innings
declared

199

hockey
hockey stick
centre

bully-off
corner
shooter
wing
foul

200

athletics
stadium
meeting
events
track
field
heats
starting gun
blocks
sprint
lanes
bend

bell
lap
back straight
finishing-line
timing
stop-watch
record
personal best
marathon
high-jump
long-jump
pit
sand
take-off
shot-put
hammer
discus
javelin
pole-vault
hurdles
steeplechase

racquet
service
let
fault
umpire
line judge
forehand
backhand
return
volley
lob
smash
slice
singles
doubles
game
set
match

201
netball
net
goal
shooter
pass
foul
court
centre

202
rounders
bat
post
base
rounder
bowler
backstop
pitch

203
swimming
pool
lanes
costume
badge
cap
dive
free-style
crawl
breast stroke
butterfly stroke
back stroke

204
tennis
court
net
racket

205
table-tennis
bat
serve
fault
return
topspin
backspin
backflip
lob
chop
smash

206
show-jumping
jumps
poles

faults
time faults
clear round
double fence
triple fence
wall
water jump
jump-off

207

motor-racing
pits
driver
starting grid
accelerate
gears
bend
corner
chicane
straight
lap
braking
breakdown
pit-stop
wheel-change
chequered flag

208

cycle racing
headgear
jersey
number
hill-climb
gears

freewheel
sponge
endurance
milk race
pursuit
sprint

209

fishing
bank
stool
rod
line
bait
hook
net
bite
strike
reel
weight
waders
fly-fishing
cast
coarse fishing
[see 116, 267]

210

golf
course
clubs
wood
iron
tee
drive

shot
fairway
bunker
green
flag
hole
putt
par
bogie
birdie
eagle

211

boxing
ring
ropes
referee
seconds
boxers
gloves
timekeeper
rounds
bell
foul
knockdown
count
points
knockout

212

wrestling
wrestlers
ropes
holds
fall

contd.

submission
knockout
catchweights
team tag
referee

213

snooker
umpire
table
baize
pockets
balls
baulk
white
reds
colours
cue
miscue
chalk
tip
break
pot
points
foul stroke
plant
frame

environment

214

universe
stars
galaxy

constellation
sun
solar system
planet
moon
axis
rotate
orbit
meteor
meteorite
comet
pulsar
quasar
nova
black hole
astronomer
observatory
telescope
reflector

215

planet Earth
ocean
continent
sea
island
archipelago
atoll
peninsula
isthmus
bight
strait
gulf
mountain
range
pass

valley
volcano
erupt
molten rock
lava
canyon
gorge
fiord
ravine
plain
grassland
prairie
steppe
pampas
forest
jungle
swamp
tundra
permafrost
icefield
icecap
glacier
iceberg
desert
sand
dune
oasis
mirage
[see 26]

216

rock
sandstone
limestone
granite
slate

chalk
shale
flint
[see 224]

217

minerals
iron
copper
tin
lead
zinc
aluminium
nickel
platinum
gold
silver
diamond
emerald
ruby
sapphire

218

country
fields
lanes
hedges
ditches
crops
trees
woods
flowers
meadows
plain

heath
moor
common
lake
pond
marsh
stream
river
hill
mountain
valley
animals
birds
insects
farms
hamlets
villages
[see 127]

219

town
city
street
road
crossing
pavement
bus
station
railway
traffic
warden
parking
car park
garage
yellow lines
policeman

contd.

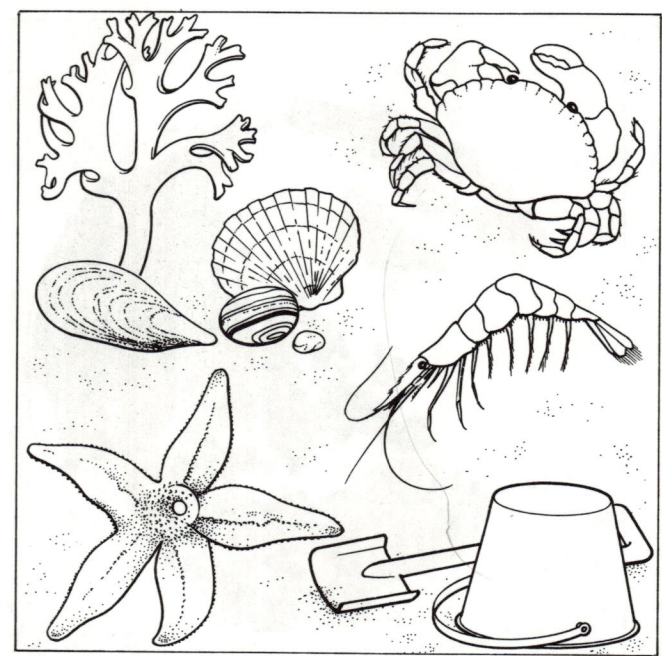

deep
swim
float
tide
current
salt
rock pool
net
catch
crab
shrimp
cockles
mussels
starfish
seaweed
beach
pebbles
shells
sandcastle
bucket
spade
picnic
deckchair
rug
sunburnt
donkey
Punch and Judy
canoe
yacht
sail
crew
pier
promenade
harbour
quay
fishing boats
[see 243-248]

department store
shop
shopping precinct
buildings
skyscraper
café
snack bar
restaurant
hotel
cinema
theatre
concert hall
town hall
church
cathedral
museum
library
bank
office
police station

fire station
hospital
ambulance depot
market
park
gardens
[see 226]

220

seaside
shore
waves
surf
breakers
paddle
splash
bathe
shallow

221

underwater
skin-diver
wetsuit
flippers
mask
aqualung
snorkel
oxygen bottle
pressure-gauge
wristwatch
compass
torch
depth
bottom
explore
rocks
reef
seaweed
wreck
sand
mud
fish
shoal
dive
swim
surface
[see 248]

222

farm
dairy
arable
stock

poultry
farmhouse
farmyard
barn
hay
straw
cowshed
milk-cooler
eggs
haystack
pigsty
trough
orchard
paddock
tractor
plough
furrow
seed
plant
manure
fertiliser
spray
crops
grain silo
silage
corn
vegetables
harvest
combine
fence
hedge
gate
animals
cattle
sheep
graze
[see 127, 128, 262]

223

mountain
range
peak
summit
cairn
rocks
cliff
scree
ridge
pass
slope
gradient
height
sheep
cloud
mist
breeze
wind
view
panorama
spring
rivulet
waterfall
[see 216]

224

river
source
spring
stream
brook
shallow
deep
flow

contd.

rapids
cataract
rocks
waterfall
meander
bank
erosion
bed
boulder
silt
weeds
rushes
salmon ladder
voles
water rats
otters
bridge
boat
ford
ferry
stepping-stones
tributary
confluence
oxbow-lake
backwater
torrent
in spate
flood
weir
mouth
estuary
[see 218, 223]

225
park
grass

shrubs
trees
shade
flowers
path
lake
swans
geese
ducks
playground
swings
bandstand
gates
[see 184, 219]

226

buildings
abbey
monastery
convent
art gallery
museum
library
swimming pool
bank
building society
cathedral
church
chapel
temple
synagogue
castle
monument
school
college
university

theatre
concert hall
cinema
department store
factory
hospital
football ground
hotel
market
office
skyscraper
palace
post office
railway station
bus station
stadium
telephone exchange
town hall
civic centre
[see 90-93, 219]

transport

227
road
street
avenue
drive
lane
by-pass
main road
trunk road
bus lane
cycle path
diversion
[see 86]

228

motorway
hard shoulder
junction
entrance
exit
service area
underpass
overpass
contra-flow
repairs
cones

229

features
T-junction
fork
crossroads
level crossing
pedestrian-crossing
zebra-crossing
pelican-crossing
roundabout
dual carriageway
traffic lights
traffic jam
tailback
layby

230

repairs
tarmac
digger
bulldozer

excavator
spreader
dumper
roadroller
roadworks
[see 129]

231

vehicle
car
saloon
taxi
limousine
sports car
racing car
estate car
hatchback
lorry
bus
coach
caravan
[see 115]

232

parts
wheels
tyres
tread
air pressure
dashboard
speedometer
radio
cassette player
stereo
windscreen
wipers
steering wheel
seat belts
boot
bonnet
radiator
headlights
dipped
main beam
fog lamps

contd.

rear lights
reversing lights
number plate
licence disc
A.A.
R.A.C.
[see 115]

petrol pumps
self-service
attendant
tank
spare parts
[see 98]

235
truck
van
lorry
tailboard
cab
tachograph
artic
articulated truck
container lorry
trailer
juggernaut
roadtanker
C.B. radio
fire-engine
ambulance
dust-cart
police car
siren
[see 87]

233
garage
filling station
petrol
gallon
litre
oil
dipstick
water
battery
charge
car wash

234
bus
single-decker
double-decker
pay-as-you-enter
bus stop
fare stage
number
destination
terminus
conductor
fare
ticket

236
motorbike
crash helmet
motorcyclist
pedals
gears
mudguards
handlebars
steer
saddle

237

animal transport
horse
pony
reins
stirrup
trot
canter
gallop
pony trek
stables
groom
harness
tackle
fodder
ox
camel
llama
donkey
mule
elephant

238

pedestrian
walk
hike
boots
anorak
rucksack
route
footpath
compass
[see 60]

239

rail
railway station
stationmaster
platform
booking office
fare
ticket
ticket-collector
inspector
baggage
luggage
freight
porter
taxi-rank
left luggage
[see 88]

240

railway journey
track
rails
sleepers
points
signals
signal box
electric
wires
bridge
viaduct
tunnel
level crossing
siding
engine sheds
turntable

241

locomotive
engine
diesel
steam
electric
pantograph
rail bus
coupling
buffers
shunting
[see 88]

242

rolling stock
carriage
coach
car
compartment
non-smoking
corridor
buffet-car
dining-car
sleeping-car
wagon
truck
brake van
guard's van
local train
commuter train
inter-city
stopping train
express

243

water transport
liner
cruise
oil tanker
cargo liner
coaster
car ferry
rowing boat
raft
lifeboat
motor boat
speedboat
powerboat
yacht
hovercraft
launch
lightship
canoe
dinghy
[see 111, 112]

244

ship
deck
bridge
cabin
porthole
bow
stern
winch
hold
cargo
funnel
smoke-stack
radio shack

anchor
propeller
screw
rudder
steer
derrick
davit
navigate
horizon
pilot
port
starboard

245

yacht
sail
rope
mast
pulley
tiller
boom
hawser
tie-up
flag
spinnaker
lifejacket

246

crew
captain
skipper
pilot
bosun
engineer
officer

seaman
coxswain
navigator
[see 116, 117]

247

port
harbour
quay
bollard
shipyard
crane
dock
dry dock
graving dock
floating dock
pier
jetty
landing-stage
alongside
loading
unloading
fork-lift truck
customs
duty
passport
[see 111, 112, 116, 117]

248

sea
ocean
tide
waves
breakers

sandbanks
rocks
channel
lighthouse
buoy
calm
rough
seasick
capsize
drown
lifebelt
[see 111, 112]

249

canal
bank
lock
lock-keeper
gate
barge
bargee
narrowboat
towpath
tunnel
swing bridge
motor-launch
houseboat
punt
canoe
paddles

250

airline
aeroplane
aircraft

airliner
helicopter
rotor
jet engine
flight
fly
flew
wings
air-brakes
fuselage
undercarriage
landing wheels
tail
fin
nose
view
fields
towns
coastline
clouds
captain
co-pilot
navigator

air hostess
steward
stewardess
galley
reclining seats
seat-belt
turbulence
lifejacket
inflate
cabin pressure
oxygen
emergency door
emergency chute

251

airport
control tower
air traffic controller
radar
terminal
customs
declare

contd.

basket
ascent
wind
altitude
drift
descent
landing

passport
security check
runway
flight path
hangar

255

space transport
rocket
capsule
shuttle
launching pad
launch
countdown
lift-off
blast-off
module
orbit
mission control

252

route
great circle
compass
distance
direction
navigate
airspeed
knots
miles
kilometres
E.T.A.
estimated time
  of arrival

253

altitude
height
climb
ascend
ascent
descend
descent
approach
radio
radar
auto-pilot

254

balloon
hot air
burn
gas
inflate

256

astronaut
cosmonaut
spacesuit
weightlessness
zero gravity
space walk
life-cord
space laboratory
space docking
satellite-launching
solar panels

257

lunar expedition
moon-track
moon-orbit
dark side
moon-landing
retro-rockets
moon-rock
moon-dust
zero atmosphere
moon-mobile
less gravity
booster-rockets
earth track
re-entry
heat shield
parachutes
touch-down
splash-down
recovery
shuttle-landing

nature

258

weather
atmosphere
stratosphere
ozone layer
clouds
cirrus
cumulus
nimbus
breeze
wind

gust
gale
whirlwind
tornado
monsoon
cyclone
anti-cyclone
typhoon
hurricane
Beaufort Scale
rain
rainbow
drizzle
shower
downpour
cloudburst
sleet
snow
blizzard
storm
thunder
lightning
frost
frozen
ice
black ice
icicle
fog
freezing fog
mist
smog

259

meteorology
meteorological
 office

barometer
barograph
air pressure
high
low
isobars
thermometer
temperature
humidity
visibility
wind gauge
rain gauge
weather vane
forecast
depression
cold front
warm front
hard frost
freezing
temperate
mild
clear
changeable
unsettled
stormy
damp
cloudy
dull
overcast
humid
fine
sunny
dry
drought
heatwave

260

temperature
hot
sweltering
blazing
searing
burning
baking
parched
steaming
boiling
blistering
torrid
scorching
sweating
tropical
oppressive
sultry
humid
clammy
close
warm
temperate
cool
chilly
keen
sharp
cold
bleak
bitter
raw
frigid
freezing
frosty
crisp
icy
frozen
glacial
arctic

261

pets
vet
veterinary
  surgeon
dog
puppy
cat
kitten
rabbit
hamster
guinea pig
gerbil
white mouse
budgerigar
parrot
pony
horse
foal
donkey
tortoise
[see 83]

262

domestic animals
sheep
ewe
ram
lamb
bull
cow
heifer
calf
calves
goat
kid
pig
hog
sow
piglet
hen
cock
[see 83]

263

**wild creatures
(Britain)**
rabbit
hare
squirrel
hedgehog
mole
fox
bat
deer
stag
badger
ferret
rat
weasel
otter
seal
adder
grass snake

264

wild creatures (overseas)
lion
tiger
leopard
cheetah
jaguar
bear
grizzly bear
polar bear
panda
koala bear
wolf
dingo
hyena
jackal
beaver
elephant
giraffe
camel
hippopotamus
rhinoceros
buffalo
bison
zebra
wildebeest
kangaroo
wallaby
reindeer
caribou
moose
antelope
gazelle
llama
gorilla

chimpanzee
orang-utan
baboon
gibbon
monkey
bush baby

thrush
robin
magpie
crow
kestrel
swallow
pigeon

265

birds (Britain)
sparrow
starling
robin
thrush
blackbird
tit
crow
rook
magpie
jackdaw
pigeon
swallow

swift
martin
wagtail
owl
cuckoo
woodpecker
finch
jay
wren
lark
duck
swan
goose
moorhen
coot
kingfisher
heron
gull
cormorant
puffin
hawk
kestrel
falcon

contd.

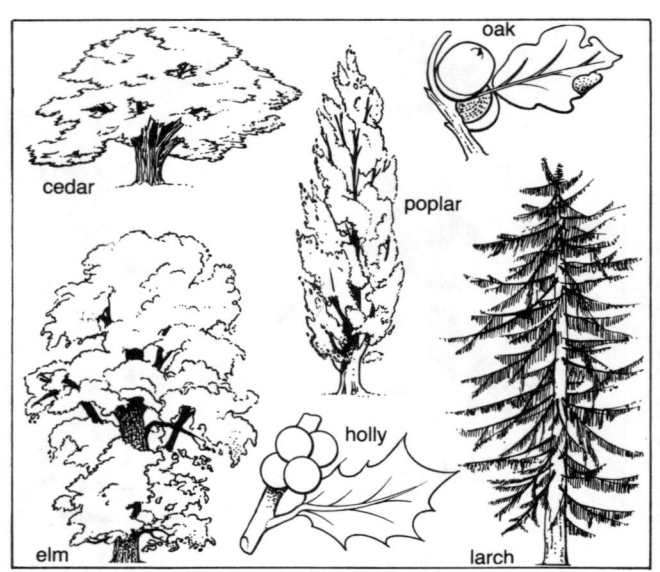

pike
roach
carp
tench
bass
bream
perch
dace
gudgeon
cod
herring
plaice
sole
haddock
halibut
mackerel
whiting
pilchard
sardine
sprat
tuna
catfish
dogfish
flounder
skate
octopus
squid
flying fish
swordfish
shark
dolphin
porpoise
whale
turtle
terrapin
crab
lobster

eagle
pheasant
grouse
partridge
quail
peacock

266

birds (overseas)
budgerigar
canary
cockatoo
macaw
parrot
mynah
parakeet
ostrich
emu
stork
crane
flamingo

cassowary
kiwi
kookaburra
lyre bird
bird of paradise
humming bird
toucan
pelican
penguin
hornbill
vulture
condor
albatross

267

water creatures
stickleback
minnow
trout
salmon
eel

shrimp
oyster
cockle
mussel
amphibian
frog
toad
newt
tadpole
salamander
[see 116, 149]

268

invertebrates
fly
blowfly
bluebottle
wasp
bee
hornet
cranefly
daddy-longlegs
butterfly
moth
caterpillar
grub
maggot
earthworm
ant
beetle
cockroach
centipede
dragonfly
ladybird
gnat
earwig

flea
louse
lice
mosquito
grasshopper
cricket
greenfly
blackfly
spider
tarantula
black widow
silkworm
praying mantis
stick insect

269

reptiles
smooth snake
grass snake
adder
viper
lizard
tortoise
slow-worm
crocodile
alligator
chameleon
iguana
python
cobra
rattlesnake
puff adder
mamba
boa constrictor
anaconda

270

trees
oak
horse chestnut
sweet chestnut
sycamore
fir
pine
elm
beech
ash
plane
lime
birch
poplar
hawthorn
willow
yew
holly
laburnum
apple
pear
plum
cherry
hazel
walnut
conifer
evergreen
deciduous
[see 184, 218, 225]

271

gardens
hedge
lawn

contd.

daisy
dandelion
border
rockery
flower-bed
path
plants
seeds
seedling
annual
perennial
fruit
orchard
flowers
cuttings
foliage
weeds
compost
manure
fertiliser
leaves
vegetables
rubbish
burn
bonfire
[see 15, 138]

272

air
oxygen
nitrogen
breathe
lungs
atmosphere
stratosphere
air pressure
barometer

bird
soar
glide
air current
ventilation
fan
draught
air-conditioning
air pump
pneumatic tyre
inflate
football
balloon
air-bed
air-brakes
aircraft
airship
aeroplane
aerosol
helicopter
autogiro
glider
kite
parachute
hovercraft
aqualung
snorkel
airtight
vacuum
suction
exhaust
windmill
wind pump
diving-bell
airlock
diver
air-line

273

water
hydrogen
oxygen
ocean
sea
tide
wave
river
stream
brook
weir
waterfall
canal
lock
pond
pool
lake

274

rain
drizzle
shower
downpour
cloudburst
flood
deluge
hail
sleet
snow
blizzard
ice
icicle
cloud
[see 258, 259]

275

mist
fog
vapour
dew
steam
sweat
condensation
evaporate
dank
humid
humidity

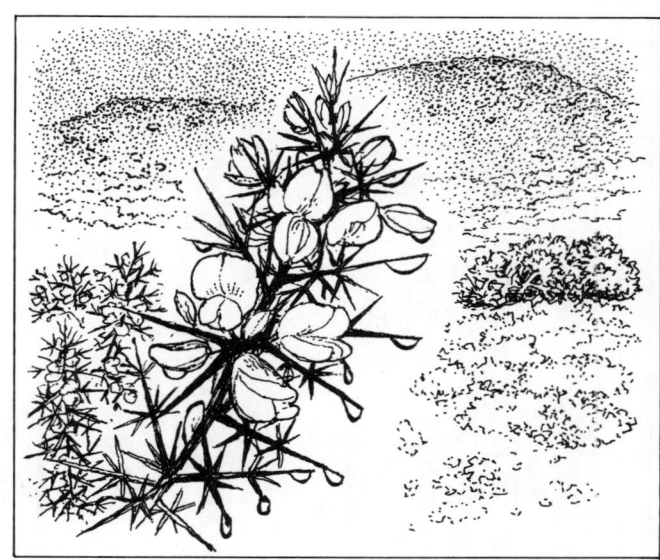

276

wet
soaked
saturated
drenched
dripping
wringing
moist
damp

277

waterworks
reservoir
dam
well
artesian
water-level
filter
purity
softening
pumping-station

fountain
jets
pipe
main
aqueduct
channel
culvert
drain
sewer
hydrant

278

domestic water
tap
tank
cistern
overflow
burst
stopcock
radiator
water-softener

hard water
soft water
water-bottle
quench
water-bed
watering-can
hose
jet
spray
[see 10, 13, 14]

279

fire
kindle
smoke
spark
smoulder
glow
flicker
burn
crackle
blaze

contd.

blazing	match	**time**
camp-fire	ignite	
bonfire	ignition	**280**
forest fire	combustion	**measurement**
beacon	conflagration	century
flame	incinerate	decade
flammable	cremate	year
non-flammable	cremation	leap year
fumes	fire-brigade	month
singe	fire-station	fortnight
melt	fireman	week
scorch	axe	weekend
char	fire-engine	day
charred	fire-hydrant	hour
ashes	fire-alarm	minute
cinders	fire-extinguisher	second
flint	siren	millisecond
friction	[see 77]	
lighter		

time

280

measurement
century
decade
year
leap year
month
fortnight
week
weekend
day
hour
minute
second
millisecond

281

season
spring
summer
autumn
winter
Christmas
New Year
Easter
Whitsun
midsummer
Halloween
equinox
solstice
bonfire night
term
half-term
holiday
annual

282

calendar
January (31 days)
February (28 or 29)
March (31)
April (30)
May (31)
June (30)
July (31)
August (31)
September (30)
October (31)
November (30)
December (31)

283

days
Sunday
Monday
Tuesday
Wednesday
Thursday
Friday
Saturday
today
yesterday
tomorrow
tonight
this morning
this afternoon
this evening
last week
this week
next week

284

daytime
daily
daybreak
dawn
sunrise
morning
noon
midday
afternoon
evening
sunset
dusk
twilight
night
midnight

285

the clock
o'clock
quarter past
half past
quarter to
chimes
Big Ben
BBC pips
fast
slow
timetable
24-hour clock
period
session
moment

286

when?
before
after
early
late
now
then
first
last
past
present
future
modern
old-fashioned
out-of-date
ancient
antique
obsolete

287

how often?
always
ever
frequently
regularly
sometimes
infrequently
occasionally
seldom
never

288

how soon?
instantly
immediately
promptly
punctually
quickly
swiftly
rapidly
speedily
suddenly
afterwards
later
some time
by and by

communications

289

language
speech
speak
talk
say
tell
relate
mention
inform
announce
describe
explain
advise
suggest
warn

order
exclaim
call
shout
yell
whisper
greet
discuss
discussion
argue
argument
converse
conversation
debate
chat
chatter
gossip
ask
request
demand
enquire
question
listen
hear

290

television
mast
studio
broadcast
producer
sound-recorder
director
floor-manager
announcer
dubbing-mixer

camera
rostrum camera
newsreader
picture
channel
colour
contrast
sound
video
aerial
station
programme
news
comedy
play
documentary
serial
musical
ballet
opera
[see 169, 187]

291

radio
transistor
receiver
portable
battery
tuner
music centre
tuning
wavelength
long wave
medium wave
short wave
frequency

F.M.
A.M.
V.H.F.
aerial
stereo
speakers
[see 168, 188]

292

telephone
mouthpiece
earpiece
call
bell
ring
answer
exchange
code
number
dial
dialling
S.T.D.
tone
engaged
cut off
disconnected
long-distance
overseas
reverse-charge call
international
cable phone
radio phone
cordless phone
satellite phone
directory
yellow pages

kiosk
coin-box
pay-phone
credit-card phone
insert
pips
emergency
999

293

letters
paper
writing
typing
envelope
address
post code
stamp
first class
second class
airmail

surface mail
franking
postmark
collection
delivery
postbox
pillar-box
by return
recorded delivery
registered post
mail van
[see 73, 161]

294

newspaper
headline
news
report
photograph
article
review

contd.

advertisement
letter
editorial
sport
cartoon
weather
crossword
stop-press
column
edition
daily
weekly
Sunday
national
provincial
local
editor
edit
reporter
journalist
contributor
photographer

delivery van
newsagent
paper-round
magazine
comic
journal
[see 105, 106]

law

295

law-making
parliament
House of Commons
House of Lords
debate
speaker
bill
act
government

cabinet
opposition
backbencher
royal assent

296

police
policeman
policewoman
C.I.D.
detective
constable
sergeant
inspector
superintendent
chief constable
police station
interview-room
caution
arrest
charge
statement
release
bail
cell
custody
[see 76]

297

court
bench
dock
witness-box
summons

case
accused
prisoner
trial
prosecute
prosecution
defend
defence
judge
magistrate
clerk of court
jury
verdict
innocent
remand
acquitted
discharged
guilty
sentence
[see 107, 108]

298

punishment
probation
fine
imprisonment
gaol
jail

299

crime
criminal
fraud
theft

thief
thieves
burglar
burglary
assault
injury
manslaughter
homicide
murder

basic descriptions

300

size (small)
infinitesimal
microscopic
minute ·
diminutive
tiny
miniature
minuscule
puny
trifling
pygmy
midget
dwarf
bonsai
undersized
stunted
shrunken
dainty
petite
minor

301

size (large)
great
huge
voluminous
elephantine
vast
lofty
tremendous
giant
massive
mighty
enormous
extensive
colossal
prodigious
gigantic
gargantuan
immense
towering
mammoth
monstrous
boundless
immeasurable
infinite

302

shape (regular)
level
straight
flat
round
curved
arched
circular

contd.

semi-circular
oval
elliptical
sphere
spherical
conical
pyramid
cylinder
cylindrical
symmetrical
balanced
square
rectangle
rectangular
triangle
triangular
hexagonal
octagonal
spiral
wavy
shapely
proportionate
upright
vertical
horizontal
diagonal
concave
convex
plane

303

shape (irregular)
bent
askew
crooked
twisted

rugged
mis-shapen
distorted
mutilated
disfigured
deformed
shapeless

304

colour
tint
hue
cast
shade
tinge
tone
bloom
pigment
dye
paint

305

dark
black
ebony
pitch
soot
jet
coal
sombre

306

light
snow
chalk

ivory
pearl
silver
cream
bleached

307

red
scarlet
crimson
vermilion
magenta
blush
blood
rose
pink
ruddy
rouge
russet
ruby
maroon

308

blue
cobalt
indigo
azure
sky
navy
ultramarine
turquoise
sapphire

309

green
jade
emerald
leaf
apple
grass
olive
sage
bottle

310

yellow
gold
lemon
topaz
primrose
buff

saffron
orange

311

brown
bronze
chestnut
tan
rust
fawn
auburn
beige

312

purple
violet
mauve
lilac

313

textures
smooth
rough
coarse
fine
fluffy
hairy
furry
prickly
sharp
blunt
jagged
spiky
serrated
indented
porous
cellular
[see 48]

INDEX

The numbers refer to the section numbers, not to the page numbers. The words and numbers which are in **bold** type are the section headings. The words and numbers which are in ordinary type are the words in the lists.

dam 277
dame 189
damp 259, 276
damson 146
dance 30, 42, 183
dandelion 271
danger 114, 135
dank 275
daring 54
dark 44, 68, **305**
Dark Ages 25
dark side
  (moon) 257
dart 42
dartboard 185
darts 185
dashboard 232
database 140
date 24
daughter 1
davit 244
dawdle 41
dawn 284
day 280, **283**
daybreak 284
daytime 284
dazzling 43
deadline 105
deafening 45
dear 181
death 5
debate 289, 295
decade 280
deceitful 70
December 282
deciduous 270
decimal 22

deck 117, 244
deckchair 220
declare 251
declared 198
decoration 8
decorator 96
deep 220, 224
deer 263
defence 108, 297
defend 24, 110, 196,
  297
defendant 108
deformed 67, 303
dejected 51
delicate 32, 67
delicious 49
delighted 50
delightful 71
deliver 179
delivery 72, 73, 87,
  179, 293
delivery van 294
deluge 274
demand 289
denims 59
dental surgeon 36
dentist 36, 80
department
  store 171, 219, 226
dependable 70
deposit 179
depot 78
depressed 51
depression 259
depth 221
deputy head 17
derrick 117, 244

descend 253
descendant 1
descent 253, 254
describe 289
desert 215
design 28
desk 18, 100, 122
dessert 144
destination 87, 234
detached 7
detective 76, 187,
  194, 296
dew 275
diagonal 302
dial 292
dialling 292
diamond 217
dictation 21
dictionary 194
died 5
diesel 132, 241
diet 32
dig 129
digestion 38
digger 230
digital
  recording 168
dim 44
diminutive 300
din 45
dinghy 243
dingo 264
dining-car 242
dining-room 9, 16
dinner 144
dinner lady 17
dipped 232

dipstick 233
direction 252
director 290
directory 292
dirt 114
dirty 71
disabled 67
disc 39, 125, 168
discharged 297
disconnected 292
discontented 52
discount 181
discouraged 51
discus 200
discuss 289
discussion 289
disease 33
disfigured 303
dish 11, 144
dishwasher 10
disinfectant 33, 104
dismal 51
dispense 82
display 84
displeased 52
distance 252
distorted 303
distressed 51
distribution 131
district nurse 81
ditch 218
divan 9
dive 203, 221
diver 272
diversion 227
divide 22
diving bell 272

divorced 4
dock 111, 116, 117,
133, 247, 297
docker 111
doctor 35, 79
document 107
documentary 290
dodge 183
dodgems 193
dog 261
dogfish 267
doll 160
doll's house 160, 185
dolphin 267
**domestic
animals 262**
domestic tools 137
domestic water 278
dominoes 185
donkey 220, 237,
261
door 7, 92, 103
doorstep 7
double bed 12
double-decker 234
double fence 206
double-glazed 7
double-glazing 92
doubles 204
downcast 51
downhearted 51
downpour 258, 274
downspout 7
downstairs 9
downy 48
drab 71
dragonfly 268

drain 7, 277
drainer 10
drank 144
draught 272
draughts 185
draw 27
drawing-board 91
drenched 276
dress 59, 175
dressing gown 61
dressing-table 12,
164
dressmaker 121
dress shop 175
dribble 196
drier 119, 173
drift 254
drill 36, 80, 89, 98,
109, 118, 132, 136
drink 144
dripping 276
drive 210, 227
driver 78, 86, 207
drizzle 258, 274
drought 259
drown 248
dry 259
drybrush 96
dry dock 247
dry goods 157
dual
carriageway 229
dubbing-mixer 290
duck 225, 265
duffel coat 58
dull 44, 71, 259
dumb 46

exclaim 289
exercise 21
exercise book 20
exhaust 272
exit 177, 189, 228
expenditure 124
expensive 181
experiment 23
explain 289
explore 221
explosion 45
express 242
extensive 301
extraction 36, 80
eye 37
eyelash 37
eyelid 37

face 37
facecloth 13
factory 226
faint 44, 46
fair 68, 69, 70, **193**
fairway 210
fairy
  godmother 189
fairy tale 194
falcon 265
fall 42, 212
fall-pipe 7
family 1
fan 272
fare 234, 239
fare stage 234
farm 72, **142**, 218,
  222
farmhouse 127, 222

farming 127
farmyard 222
fascinated 56
fashionable 71
fast 42, 285
fasteners 64
fat 67, 143, 150
father 1
father-in-law 2
fault 204, 205, 206
fawn 311
fear 53
fearful 53
fearless 54
feather duster 137
February 282
fed-up 52
feeble 32
feet 60
fence 7, 222
fender 9
ferret 263
ferry 111, 224
fertiliser 15, 222,
  271
fetid 47
feverish 32
fibreglass 14
fiction 126, 194
field 127, 184, 200,
  218, 250
fielder 198
fifteen 197
fight 110
figures 22
file 122, 136
filling 36, 80

filling station 233
film 162, 191
filter 277
fin 250
finch 265
fine 259, 298, 313
finger 37, 149
finish 207
finishing-line 200
fiord 215
fir 270
fire 77, 279
fire-alarm 279
fire-blanket 77
fire-brigade 279
fire-engine 77, 235,
  279
fire-extinguisher 77,
  279
fire guard 77
fire hydrant 279
fireman 77, 279
fireplace 9
fire-station 77, 219,
  279
firm 48
first 286
first-aid 78
first class 293
fish 149, 221
fisherman 116
fishing 209
fishing boat 220
fit 32
fitted kitchen 10
fitter 109
fitting 115, 121

frozen food   163
frozen
  vegetables   145
fruit   146, 271
fruit juice   151
fry   102, 152
fuel   103, 170
full   182
full stop   21
full-time   196
fume   279
funeral   5
funnel   244
furious   52
furniture   164
furrow   222
furry   313
fuse   97, 167
fuselage   250
future   286

galaxy   214
gale   258
galleria   178
galley   250
gallon   233
gallop   237
game   30, 160, 183,
  204
gantry   112
gaol   298
garage   7, 219, **233**
garden   15, 16, **138,**
  219, **271**
gardener   17
gargantuan   301
garlic   145

gas   10, **134,** 254
gas-cooled   135
gas fire   9
gas fitter   99
gas holder   134
gate   7, 103, 222,
  225, 249
gauge   98
gaunt   67
gazelle   264
gear   207, 208, 236
geese   225
general   32, 197
generator   131
gentle   70
gentlemen   173
geography   26
gerbil   261
germ   33
get well   172
giant   301
gibbon   264
gift-wrap   182
gigantic   301
gin   176
giraffe   264
glacial   260
glacier   215
glad   50
glaring   43
glass   9, 13
glassware   123
gleaming   43
glide   272
glider   272
glittering   43
globe   20, 26

gloomy   51
gloss paint   95
glossy   43, 48
gloves   58, 174, 198,
  211
glow   279
glowing   43
glue   28
gnat   268
goal   195, 201
goalkeeper   196
goalpost   196
goat   262
gold   217, 310
golden   69
golf   210
goods   84
goose   265
gooseberry   146
gorge   215
gorilla   264
gossip   289
government   295
gown   59
grades   133
gradient   223
grain silo   222
gram   22
grammar   21
grandchild   1
granddaughter   1
grandfather   1
grandmother   1
grandparents   1
grandson   1
granite   216
grape   146

graph 22
grass 15, 225, 309
grasshopper 268
grassland 215
grass snake 263,
   269
grate 9
gratified 50
graving dock 247
gravy 152
graze 222
greasy 48
great 301
great circle 252
green 210, **309**
greenfly 268
greenhouse 15
greet 289
greeting 172
grey 69
grief-stricken 51
grill 10, 102
grilled 152
grinder 11
gripped 56
grizzly bear 264
groceries 150
grocery 157
groom 237
ground 198
group 19
grouse 265
grub 268
guard 88
guard's van 242
gudgeon 267
guest 4

guilty 108, 297
guinea pig 261
guitar 31
gulf 215
gull 265
gums 36
gusher 118
gust 258
gutter 7

haddock 149, 267
hail 274
hair 37, **69**
hair cream 173
haircut 173
hairdresser 119, 173
hairstyle 173
hairy 48, 313
hake 149
half-brother 1
half past 285
half-sister 1
half-term 281
half-time 196
halibut 267
hall 9, 16, 190
Halloween 281
ham 148, 158
hamburger 148
hamlet 218
hammer 89, 136,
   200
hamster 261
hand 37
handlebars 236
handrail 9
handstand 30

hang 96
hangar 251
Hanoverian 25
happy 50
happy ending 189
harbour 117, 220,
   247
hard 48
hard frost 259
hard hat 114, 118
hard shoulder 228
hardware 125, 140
hard water 278
hare 263
harness 237
harrow 142
harvest 127, 222
hat 62, 174
hatchback 231
hawk 265
hawser 245
hawthorn 270
hay 222
hay fever 33
haystack 222
hay whisk 142
hazel 270
hazel nut 146
head 37, **62**
header 196
headgear 208
headlights 232
headline 294
headmaster 17, 101
headmistress 17,
   101
head's room 16

Terylene 66
test 21, 23
testing 115
textbook 20, 194
texture 313
thatch 7
**theatre 34,
    189**, 219, 226
theft 299
then 286
theodolite 90
thermometer 23, 33,
    259
thermostat 10
thick 48
thickset 67
thief 299
thieves 299
thigh-bone 39
thin 48, 67
thirteen 197
this afternoon 283
this evening 283
this morning 283
this week 283
thread 29
three-piece suite 9
thrilled 55
thrush 265
thumb 37
thunder 45, 258
Thursday 283
ticket 86, 234, 239
ticket-collector 88,
    239
tide 220, 248, 273
tie 63, 174

tie-pin 63
tie-up 245
tiger 264
tightrope 192
tights 59, 175
tile 7, 8
till 84, 163, 180
tiller 245
time 24
time fault 206
time keeper 211
timetable 19, 285
timid 53
timing 200
tin 157, 217
tinge 304
tint 119, 304
tiny 67, 300
tip 154, 213
tired 57
tit 265
title 194
T-junction 31, 229
toad 267
toasted 152
toaster 11, 141
tobacco 85, 170
tobacconist 170
today 283
toddle 41
toe 37
toffee 159
toggle 64
toilet 13, 94
toilet articles 162
token 86
tomato 145, 146

tomorrow 283
tone 292, 304
tongs 9
tongue 37, 148
tonight 283
tonne 22
tonsilitis 33
tool 165
toolshed 15
toothbrush 13
toothpaste 13
topaz 310
topple 41
top spin 205
torch 221
tornado 258
torrent 224
torrid 260
tortoise 261, 269
totter 41
toucan 266
touch 48, 197, 203
touch-down 257
tousled 69
towel 13
towering 301
town 219, 250
town hall 226
towpath 249
toyshop 160
trace element 143
track 200, 240
tractor 142, 222
traffic 219
traffic jam 229
traffic lights 229
tragedy 189